Essential resources for training and HR professionals

GLOBAL EXECUTIVE
LEADERSHIP
INVENTORY

Manfred F. R. Kets de Vries

OBSERVER

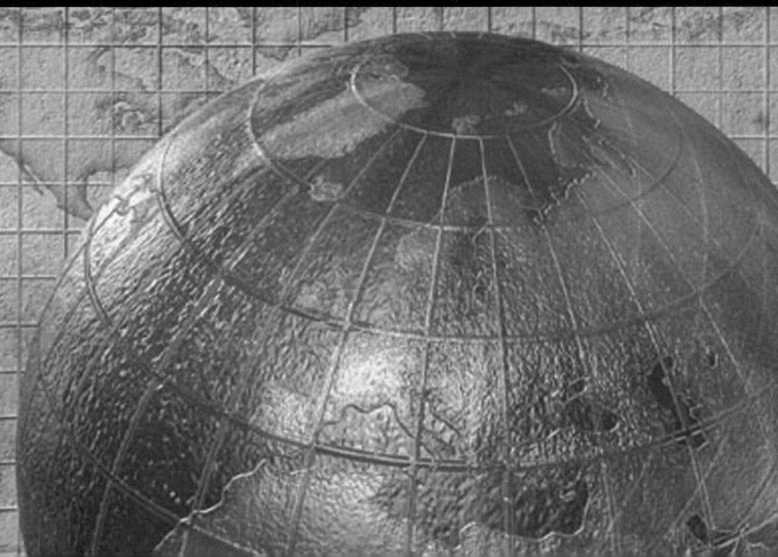

Before you complete this questionnaire, please read the following instructions carefully.

Excellent global leadership comes from a set of competencies in several different dimensions. The *Global Executive Leadership Inventory* is designed to help Leaders reflect on their leadership behaviors and compare their self-perceptions to those of outside Observers, as well as to those of a reference group of very high achievers, many of whom are CEOs of global organizations.

Here are some points to keep in mind when completing the questionnaire:

- There are no right or wrong answers, and there are no "trick" questions.

- For the results to be useful, it is important that you answer honestly and openly, to the best of your knowledge. Please indicate what you think the Leader ACTUALLY DOES, not what you think he or she should be doing.

- Answer all the questions quickly, and don't worry about whether your responses are consistent from item to item.

- Answer ALL the questions. The questionnaire can only be scored correctly if all the questions are answered.

- You might find the last group of questions (81–100) difficult to answer because they address the Leader's personal life. For these questions, you have the option of selecting "not observed." Please use that option as a last resort. In 360-degree feedback surveys, it is perceptions that count, and your perceptions are extremely important for the Leader.

HOW TO ANSWER QUESTIONS 1–89

Indicate the degree to which each statement describes the way you think that the Leader acts in a particular situation. The higher the rating, the more accurately the statement describes the Leader's behavior. For example:

This rating: Means this:

1   The statement does not describe the Leader's behavior at all—as far as you know, he or she NEVER acts in the way that is described, implying that the person is deficient in this area.

4   The statement describes the way the Leader acts SOME OF THE TIME—you feel that he or she is as competent as, but not outstanding, when compared with other Leaders in this area.

7   The statement accurately describes the way the Leader acts ALL THE TIME—as far as you know, he or she ALWAYS acts in the way that is described, implying that the person's behavior in this area is exemplary.

NOTE: Please keep these nuances in mind while answering these questions. Most Leaders are excellent in many areas, but not all.

Name of Leader_____

I (the Observer) am this Leader's: ○ Superior   ○ Coworker   ○ Direct Report   ○ Other

This person:	Not at all 1	2	3	4	5	6	Very well 7
1. actively encourages new business opportunities.	○	○	○	○	○	○	○
2. often challenges the status quo.	○	○	○	○	○	○	○
3. is actively involved in defining strategy.	○	○	○	○	○	○	○
4. when making decisions, considers the whole situation rather than the details only.	○	○	○	○	○	○	○
5. finds ways to simplify complex situations for employees.	○	○	○	○	○	○	○
6. considers how future events will affect his/her organization.	○	○	○	○	○	○	○
7. is open to new ways of doing things.	○	○	○	○	○	○	○
8. inspires people to look beyond existing limitations.	○	○	○	○	○	○	○
9. makes sure that all employees have a clear idea of where the organization is going.	○	○	○	○	○	○	○
10. tries to involve employees in decision making.	○	○	○	○	○	○	○
11. encourages people to make their own decisions.	○	○	○	○	○	○	○
12. does everything in his/her power to create commitment to the organization.	○	○	○	○	○	○	○
13. tolerates mistakes made by employees who are taking the initiative.	○	○	○	○	○	○	○
14. encourages people to share information within the organization.	○	○	○	○	○	○	○
15. tries to minimize secrecy within his/her organization.	○	○	○	○	○	○	○
16. once he/she has delegated a task, lets the person in charge take full responsibility.	○	○	○	○	○	○	○
17. has an action-oriented leadership style.	○	○	○	○	○	○	○
18. makes people aware that he/she is available for them.	○	○	○	○	○	○	○
19. conveys his/her ideas in a clear and understandable way.	○	○	○	○	○	○	○
20. shows enthusiasm for projects.	○	○	○	○	○	○	○
21. is an important source of motivation for his/her people.	○	○	○	○	○	○	○
22. mobilizes people to get things done.	○	○	○	○	○	○	○
23. tries to be a role model for his/her people.	○	○	○	○	○	○	○
24. makes an effort to interact with people at all levels of the organization.	○	○	○	○	○	○	○
25. sets clear performance standards and goals for his/her people.	○	○	○	○	○	○	○
26. works to develop organizational systems that reflect corporate values.	○	○	○	○	○	○	○
27. makes sure that performance standards are adhered to.	○	○	○	○	○	○	○
28. makes sure that management systems facilitate effective behavior.	○	○	○	○	○	○	○
29. makes people accountable for their commitments and deadlines.	○	○	○	○	○	○	○
30. emphasizes corporate values that serve to unite people in his/her organization.	○	○	○	○	○	○	○
31. ensures that people respect the basic values of his/her corporate culture.	○	○	○	○	○	○	○

	Not at all						Very well
	1	2	3	4	5	6	7
32. uses various types of incentives to compensate his/her people.	○	○	○	○	○	○	○
33. makes sure that compensation for employees is fair and reflects individual efforts.	○	○	○	○	○	○	○
34. makes sure that an employee's performance review is a summary of ongoing feedback.	○	○	○	○	○	○	○
35. spends time mentoring others in his/her organization.	○	○	○	○	○	○	○
36. makes sure that outstanding performance is rewarded appropriately.	○	○	○	○	○	○	○
37. gives ongoing constructive feedback to his/her people.	○	○	○	○	○	○	○
38. makes sure that people's achievements are recognized.	○	○	○	○	○	○	○
39. gives feedback with respect.	○	○	○	○	○	○	○
40. tries to resolve conflict among team members in a way that strengthens the team.	○	○	○	○	○	○	○
41. encourages team members to build collaborative relationships with one another.	○	○	○	○	○	○	○
42. when on a team, puts the interest of the group before his/her own personal goals.	○	○	○	○	○	○	○
43. builds on team members' individual strengths.	○	○	○	○	○	○	○
44. makes a great effort to earn the trust of other team members.	○	○	○	○	○	○	○
45. looks for a variety of personality types when forming a team.	○	○	○	○	○	○	○
46. makes a serious effort to ensure that, when a decision is made, everyone stands behind it.	○	○	○	○	○	○	○
47. tries to make sure that all members of the group feel that they contribute to the decision-making process.	○	○	○	○	○	○	○
48. welcomes differences of opinion.	○	○	○	○	○	○	○
49. looks for solutions to problems that are satisfactory to most parties.	○	○	○	○	○	○	○
50. when possible, includes people from different regional/national cultures and genders in teams he/she creates.	○	○	○	○	○	○	○
51. makes sure that everyone on his/her team recognizes the importance of knowing and meeting customers' requirements.	○	○	○	○	○	○	○
52. makes sure that customer satisfaction is the focus of the team's efforts.	○	○	○	○	○	○	○
53. makes sure that customers, suppliers, and other stakeholders are treated fairly.	○	○	○	○	○	○	○
54. encourages effective interaction with outside stakeholders.	○	○	○	○	○	○	○
55. ensures that his/her organization makes positive contributions to the communities around it.	○	○	○	○	○	○	○
56. keeps himself/herself informed about global developments that might affect the organization's business.	○	○	○	○	○	○	○
57. is aware of the ways in which cultural differences affect the way people behave.	○	○	○	○	○	○	○
58. is comfortable in situations where the culture is unfamiliar to him/her.	○	○	○	○	○	○	○
59. enjoys working on multicultural teams.	○	○	○	○	○	○	○

	Not at all				Very well		
	1	**2**	**3**	**4**	**5**	**6**	**7**
60. assumes that no culture is better than another.	○	○	○	○	○	○	○
61. enjoys learning and speaking foreign languages.	○	○	○	○	○	○	○
62. makes cross-cultural experiences into learning opportunities for himself/herself.	○	○	○	○	○	○	○
63. is good at adapting to business practices in cultures other than his/her own.	○	○	○	○	○	○	○
64. has a set of principles that he/she defends.	○	○	○	○	○	○	○
65. is prepared to stick to an unpopular decision if he/she feels that it is the right one.	○	○	○	○	○	○	○
66. is willing to take risks when he/she strongly believes in a certain action.	○	○	○	○	○	○	○
67. is not easily discouraged.	○	○	○	○	○	○	○
68. when he/she believes it is necessary, tries to change the opinions of others.	○	○	○	○	○	○	○
69. considers how his/her emotions can affect others.	○	○	○	○	○	○	○
70. can "read" other people's feelings quite well.	○	○	○	○	○	○	○
71. understands the reasons why he/she feels the way he/she does in a particular situation.	○	○	○	○	○	○	○
72. analyzes his/her feelings before acting on them.	○	○	○	○	○	○	○
73. makes sure that his/her behavior is appropriate to the situation.	○	○	○	○	○	○	○
74. analyzes his/her mistakes in order to learn from them.	○	○	○	○	○	○	○
75. engages in an ongoing process of self-reflection.	○	○	○	○	○	○	○
76. when someone is talking to him/her, gives the person his/her full attention.	○	○	○	○	○	○	○
77. makes a great effort to help people feel at ease with him/her.	○	○	○	○	○	○	○
78. actively shows his/her respect for and interest in individuals.	○	○	○	○	○	○	○
79. tries to generate trust among the people he/she works with.	○	○	○	○	○	○	○
80. gets people to open up by being easily approachable.	○	○	○	○	○	○	○

	Not Observed	Not at all				Very well		
		1	**2**	**3**	**4**	**5**	**6**	**7**
81. apparently takes the time to think about his/her life on a regular basis.	○	○	○	○	○	○	○	○
82. looks for opportunities to learn more about himself/herself.	○	○	○	○	○	○	○	○
83. actively looks for new ideas and learning opportunities outside of his/her specific field of expertise.	○	○	○	○	○	○	○	○
84. is physically active (regular exercise).	○	○	○	○	○	○	○	○
85. engages in non-work-related activities (such as sports, hobbies, or volunteer activities) at least once a week.	○	○	○	○	○	○	○	○
86. has at least one close friend with whom he/she can talk about very personal issues.	○	○	○	○	○	○	○	○

	Not Observed	Not at all						Very well
		1	2	3	4	5	6	7
87. frequently spends time with his/her spouse/partner and/or other close family members.	○	○	○	○	○	○	○	○
88. appears to have caring and trusting relationships with his/her spouse/partner and/or other close family members.	○	○	○	○	○	○	○	○
89. sets priorities in both his/her private and professional lives.	○	○	○	○	○	○	○	○

HOW TO ANSWER QUESTIONS 90–100

Answer these questions according to your feelings or perceptions. In this case, a score of 1 means that, as far as you know, the Leader has no problems in that area. A score of 7 means that the Leader obviously has problems in the area, based on what you feel or know to be true.

	Not Observed	Never						Always
		1	2	3	4	5	6	7
90. appears to feel that his/her workload is too heavy.	○	○	○	○	○	○	○	○
91. never seems to be able to complete all the work he/she has to do.	○	○	○	○	○	○	○	○
92. feels that the pressure at work has become excessively stressful.	○	○	○	○	○	○	○	○
93. seems to feel that his/her career is not progressing the way he/she would like it to.	○	○	○	○	○	○	○	○
94. appears to have too many responsibilities.	○	○	○	○	○	○	○	○
95. says that he/she has little control over the things that happen to him/her.	○	○	○	○	○	○	○	○
96. appears to be currently worried about his/her own health.	○	○	○	○	○	○	○	○
97. worries about the health of one or more close family members.	○	○	○	○	○	○	○	○
98. is worried about his/her financial situation.	○	○	○	○	○	○	○	○
99. has a relationship with one or more close family members that is a source of stress.	○	○	○	○	○	○	○	○
100. doesn't seem to be managing his/her career in an effective manner.	○	○	○	○	○	○	○	○

In order to become more effective as a Leader, what behavior does the person you are rating need to continue, develop, and/or eliminate?

CONTINUE

Please describe two or three behavioral patterns that contribute to the person's effectiveness as a Leader (for example, "Makes an effort to give constructive feedback to subordinates").

DEVELOP

Please describe two or three behavioral patterns that the person could improve (for example, "Run more focused and organized meetings").

ELIMINATE

Please describe two or three behavioral patterns that the person should eliminate to be more effective as a Leader (for example, "Stop micromanaging the work he/she delegates").

ADDITIONAL COMMENTS

Please use this space to give the Leader additional feedback on his or her leadership behavior.

ISBN:978-0-787-97418-3

90000

9 780787 974183